Family Outings

Family Outings

A Play About Relationships
in Three Acts, a Prologue, and an Epilogue

by Paul McCusker

Author of *Catacombs*
and *Vantage Points*

A Lillenas Drama Resource

Lillenas Publishing Co.
KANSAS CITY, MO. 64141

PLEASE READ CAREFULLY

This is a royalty play. Permission to perform this work is granted upon the payment of a licensing fee of $25.00 for the first nonprofit performance and $15.00 for each subsequent performance, whether or not admission is charged. Please send your check to the above address with the following information: Your Name, Organization, Address, Play title, Number of intended performances, and Amount remitted.

Permission and royalty information for performance for profit or by professionals must be secured from the publisher: Lillenas Publishing Co., P.O. Box 419527, Kansas City, MO 64141.

The writing of plays is a means of livelihood, and playwrights depend upon production for support. Support Christian drama by supporting its creator—the playwright.

Family Outings was originally written for the nationally acclaimed Jeremiah People, a Christian touring company dedicated to using comedy, drama, and music as tools to edify and challenge today's Christians. In keeping with Jeremiah People's approach, my desire was to write a program that took an uncompromising look at the problems that can tear a family apart and the work it takes to hold it together. No pat answers. No pie-in-the-sky solutions. No cute bows tying everything up at the end. I wanted the hard realities of life combined with the hope for personal change only Christ can bring through obedient hearts. Easy to say, harder to do. But that's the challenge for all of us.

The set used by Jeremiah People was an example of versatility; a necessity for a group traveling to churches throughout the United States and Canada. For the prologue, Roger Ambrose, the designer, produced a city skyline on a canvas that was attached with Velcro and covered the main cabin set. During the blackout for the taped dialogue (the drive to the cabin), cast members pulled the canvas down. The cabin set consisted primarily of the walls and fireplace painted on canvas that was tied to large attachable hollow tubes held upright by microphone stands. The furniture was created by putting folding chairs together and covering them with cloth and cushions. Of course, the set isn't the priority here. According to your church's architectural design, you can make it as elaborate or as simple as you want (or can afford). Let common sense mixed with creativity prevail. A well-crafted set will enhance good performance but will not cover bad acting. And a poorly done set will take away from everything. As far as I'm concerned, the priority is to present believable characters.

This published version of *Family Outings* is the result of a year "on the road" with Jeremiah People. Beyond the original script, I've incorporated lines and bits of characterization the cast members discovered as they performed night after night. I've also restored some of the lines that were edited along the way because of Jeremiah People's time constraints.

Heartfelt gratitude must be expressed to Chuck Bolte—producer, collaborator, and friend. His ongoing input was crucial to the development of every aspect of this play. I am also appreciative of the talent and creativity that each member of Jeremiah People brought to their roles, on and off stage. They were:

Jim Custer
Carol Hamilton
David Perona
Missy Maxwell
Steve Wunch
Rene Raines
J. R. Nisley

Also, Neal Richardson, Artie Autry, Leesa Bellesi for her oustanding choreography, Tim Hosman and Bob Hoose who participated in its early dramatic direction.

I am also indebted to Paul Miller, my editor at Lillenas, for his belief in this work and for continuing to be an innovative force in Christian drama publishing. I'm proud to consider him a friend, as well.

Other Works by the Author

Vantage Points (Lillenas), *Catacombs* (Lillenas), *Youth Ministry Drama & Comedy* (Grove), *Pap's Place* (Lillenas), *A Time for Christmas,** *The Case of the Frozen Saints* (Baker's Plays), *The Meaning of Life & Other Vanities* with Tim Albritton (Baker's Plays), *Just Between Friends,** *The Faded Flower Christmas Show,** *The Pearly Gates,** *A Small Concoction* with Tim Albritton,* *Batteries Not Included* (Baker's Plays), *The Waiting Room* (Baker's Plays), *A Homemade Christmas,** *Camp W,** *The First Church of Pete's Garage* (Baker's Plays), *Home for Christmas* (Baker's Plays), *Souvenirs* (Baker's Plays), *Sketches of Harvest* (Baker's Plays), *Spinning**

*Currently unpublished. Available from the author.

Family Outings

A Play About Relationships
in Three Acts, a Prologue, and an Epilogue

Cast of Characters:

AUNT MATTY: Should be played sensitively as an eccentric woman who has seen a lot of life in her many years of living in a small town. She is down-home and strong. Her quirksome personality shouldn't be misinterpreted as foolish; she carries a lot of fundamental wisdom.

JIM BAILEY: Without resorting to any particular stereotypes, Jim embodies a fairly typical middle-aged, middle-class husband and father who is struggling to hold on to his family and bring it a little closer to what he thinks it should be.

CHARLIE BAILEY: Like Jim, she is a fairly typical middle-aged, middle-class wife and mother who, in lieu of a career, has busied herself with a number of church and civic activities. She is a woman of strong and very practical sensibilities.

MARK BAILEY: Mark, the youngest son, is a teenager who is going through transitions. Yet, he should never be rendered as an irresponsible high schooler. Behind his glib humor is a very serious young man struggling to find his own identity amid the family's problems.

DAVID BAILEY: The oldest son, David captures the idealistic romanticism of a young man in love and, later, the bewildered disillusionment when things don't work out the way he thought they would.

BETH: She is David's equal as an idealistic romantic who sees her husband-to-be as a "Knight in Shining Armor." Later, when the armor proves to have a few kinks in it, she must adjust to life as it really is.

SAMSON: Terminally shy and quiet, Samson is Mark's age and should be played with silent comic timing without appearing stupid.

LEWIS & BICKWOOD: WCOW's team of disc jockeys who should banter with the warmth and friendliness as only small-town disc jockeys can.

Scene Descriptions:

Prologue—A limbo area with chairs arranged as a family station wagon.

Act One
Scene 1—Interior of dilapidated mountain cabin
Scene 2—That night in the same cabin
Scene 3—Much later that same night

Act Two
Scene 1—Christmas Eve in the cabin
Scene 2—Later that night at the cabin; fishing hole area downstage

Act Three
Scene 1—Spring at the cabin; it's nearly Easter
Scene 2—Later the same day

Epilogue—The cabin one week later

Prologue

(MATTY *enters into a spotlight. Well into her monologue, the lights come up on six chairs set up to simulate a car [station wagon, to be precise]. Behind the chairs and around them are assorted suitcases—ultimately to be placed behind the last row of chairs [the back of the wagon] as part of the stage "busyness." It is summer, sometime in June.)*

MATTY: Y'know, it's funny to me how things just don't seem to work out the way you think they will. No, sirree. In fact, they often—*(Interrupts herself.)* Oh, I'm sorry. It's terribly rude of me to start talking without introducing myself. My name is Matty. Aunt Matty, folks around here call me. You see, I first met the Bailey family—oh, it was two summers ago. I know that because I helped Doc Fisher in his office two summers ago. I was working there and Ted Johnson came in after trying to clean the poison ivy out from under his porch. You'd think by now he'd know to dress more thoroughly before he did that. Well, Ted Johnson's sitting there looking like a bad raspberry and he tells me that his son Dale, who sells real estate, was up visiting the weekend before and said that he finally sold Old Willard's cabin. Now that's quite a miracle if you know the place. Even for Dale. And Dale could sell ear plugs to a deaf man, if you know what I mean. Willard, you see, was a particularly unhappy man who took off the year before to live with his daughter. So the cabin sat for a year until Dale Johnson sold it, and that's how I met the Bailey family. So, you see, things don't work out the way you think they will—at least they didn't for the Baileys—somethin' you'll see in a minute just as soon as I shut up and get on with this thing . . .

(JIM *enters—happy, enthusiastic—carrying more luggage to add to what is already seen on the stage.)*

JIM: OK, let's go! We don't want to get caught in traffic! *(To himself as he looks at the luggage)* What is all this junk? *(As he asks himself that question,* CHARLIE, *his wife, has entered behind him, studiously going over a clipboard.* JIM *turns and shouts for her—and winds up doing it right in her face.)* Charlie!

CHARLIE *(jumping back):* Hello.

JIM: Oh. I'm sorry. Can we discuss this overabundance of luggage, please? This is a weekend trip!

CHARLIE: Jim, dear, you won't tell me where we're going so I didn't know how to pack. Tell me where we're going and I'll be happy to rearrange the luggage.

JIM: You're an extortionist, and it won't work. It's a surprise. You don't want me to spoil the surprise, do you? *(He busies himself with getting the luggage loaded.)*

CHARLIE: In a word . . . yes. I don't like surprises. Especially when you've masterminded them.

JIM: Now what's that supposed to mean?

CHARLIE: Darling, think back over the course of our marriage—all 22 years of it. Every time you've tried to surprise me, it has had catastrophic results.

JIM: Catastrophic? I don't remember any catastrophics.

CHARLIE: The swimming pool. Have you forgotten that?

JIM *(quietly)*: No.

CHARLIE: Some men send flowers for birthdays. Some men buy candy. But you send a bulldozer to start digging up the backyard for a swimming pool— after we agreed we couldn't afford it.

JIM: The company gave me a bargain.

CHARLIE: Nice of them to do that before they skipped town.

JIM: It's the thought that counts.

CHARLIE: I wish you'd never had the thought. You're a sucker, Jim. You're a con man's fantasy.

JIM: Don't worry. We'll get it finished one day.

CHARLIE: Sure we will. But until then I'm the only woman in town with a moat.

JIM: It isn't that bad.

CHARLIE: Did you know that Mark wanted to open it up for mud-wrestling competition?

JIM: Mark has always been an industrious lad. *(Beat.)* But this is a good surprise, Charlie. You'll love this. Listen, you're the one who's always concerned about finances, right? You're always talking about how we spend too much on vacations. This is a way for us to have a vacation without paying a fortune. In fact, we can vacation as often as we want, and it'll barely cost us a cent.

CHARLIE: That's what scares me. There's no such thing as a vacation that barely costs a cent. Why do we have to take a vacation at all? Why can't we vacation right here at home?

JIM: Because we don't stay home. David and Mark are always running, and between your church committees, organizations, and classes, we—

DAVID *(offstage)*: Mom! Telephone! It's Mrs. Hendricks.

CHARLIE (*shouting back*): All right! (*Looks at clipboard*) I was supposed to call her. (*Begins to move away to exit*)

JIM (*speaking to her as she exits*): See? We need to leave. It's the only time we get to be together as a family!

CHARLIE: You're exaggerating. We're together a lot. You're just overreacting to—

DAVID (*offstage*): Mom! She says it's important.

CHARLIE (*groans, gestures to hold the thought*): Let me talk to Mrs. Hendricks. (*Exits*)

(MARK *enters dressed in a "Rambo" outfit—that is, he's wearing military fatigues and accessories appropriate for jungle fighting. He is carrying a matching knapsack, which he drops casually then turns to exit again.* JIM *watches him for a moment.*)

JIM: Mark.

MARK: Yeah?

JIM: Field maneuvers aren't on the agenda for this weekend.

MARK: You're a funny man, Dad. (*Turns to exit*)

JIM: Mark. (MARK *turns to him again.*) Son, why are you dressed like this?

MARK: Like what?

JIM: Like you're about to take hostages.

MARK: Come on, Dad. This is the look.

JIM: The look? The look for what?

MARK: How am I supposed to know? I'm just the mindless consumer who follows the fashion trends.

JIM: Where's your brother?

MARK: He and Beth are sumo wrestling on the couch—as usual.

JIM: Well, clang the bell and have them go to their corners. I need their luggage out here. We're running late.

MARK (*moving to exit*): Y'know, I'll be glad when they get married and get into their own place. Their behavior isn't healthy for me. (*Exits*)

JIM: It's not healthy for them, either. (*Begins loading luggage into the car*) One man's family. You try to get them to take a vacation and what happens? You stand in the driveway talking to yourself.

(DAVID *and* BETH *enter again with their luggage—they are hanging all over each other affectionately.*)

JIM: Thank you. Please get the rest of the luggage loaded. That should keep your hands busy for a while. I'll make sure we're not missing anything. *(Looks at them again before he exits)* Sometimes young love is enough to make me throw up.

(JIM exits.)

BETH: Your father is taking this weekend pretty seriously.

DAVID: Yeah. He's been reading all these books about the family. I guess he thinks this is a good way to put some of the principles into practice.

(Silence for a moment as DAVID loads luggage. BETH is obviously considering what she is about to say.)

BETH: David, rather than go this weekend, why don't we just slip away and get married *now?*

DAVID: You don't get any presents that way.

BETH: I don't care. I don't care about any of it. Let's skip the vacation and go get married.

DAVID: We have to wait.

BETH: I'm tired of waiting. This engagement feels like it's lasted an eternity.

DAVID: It's only been a couple of months. And in four months the dastardly deed will be done.

BETH: I won't make it.

DAVID: We have to.

BETH: I'm so sick of the arrangements, the dresses, the invitations . . .

DAVID: We've been round and round about this already. You have to be patient.

BETH: Being patient takes too much time!

DAVID: Let me write that down. (DAVID *takes her in his arms again.)* Relax, darling, we'll make it. *(As he moves to kiss her, MARK enters.)*

MARK *(disgusted):* They're at it again. When do you two find time to breathe?

DAVID: Take notes, little man.

(DAVID kisses BETH again.)

MARK: I wish you'd stop it. I'm still an impressionable young boy.

(JIM and CHARLIE enter hurriedly.)

CHARLIE: Jim, I need the phone number for where we'll be. They're deciding tonight on the new Ladies Auxiliary treasurer at church, and I want Edna to call—

JIM: No.

CHARLIE: "No" because you don't have the number, or "no" because you're not going to give it to me?

JIM: Just no. *(As a grand announcement to all)* Now, get this clear because we're going to get in the car and go away from here and spend time together as a family should, and we're going to enjoy ourselves whether we like it or not! The world will have to rotate on its axis without you for 48 hours. Do you think it'll make it? I do. I want everyone to understand that this is a *family* vacation—short as it may be. Do you think we can do that for one weekend? What do you say, huh? *(To DAVID)* David?

DAVID *(hesitantly)*: Sure we can.

MARK *(trying to appease his father's outburst)*: Yeah, sure, Dad. Whatever you want.

JIM: Great. Let's get going. *(They begin climbing into the "car." DAVID and BETH are tickling each other.)* You two behave, or I'll put Mark between you.

MARK: Oh, please, no. They'll drool all over me.

JIM: OK, let's go! We've wasted enough time! Are we all settled? Everyone has everything? Mark, you haven't left anything on in your room—like your stereo or television or computer?

MARK: Why do you always assume my stuff gets left on?

JIM: Are you kidding? The man from the electric company suggested putting a separate meter on your room alone. We're set, then. We've got our luggage?

ALL: Check.

JIM: Food?

ALL: Check.

JIM: Everyone's gone to the bathroom?

ALL *(but JIM)*: Uh oh.

(Everyone scrambles out of the car and exits—leaving JIM to look at the audience with exasperation.)

(Blackout.)

ACT ONE
Scene One

(Before the lights come up, we hear, taped, the sound of the station wagon's motor and the voices of the characters.)

MARK: Come on, Dad, we've been riding around these mountains for hours. Where are we going?

JIM: All right . . . I know you're going to be excited. *(Speaks as if stating something of great significance)* We're going to a cabin.

(Silence.)

MARK: A cabin? What are we going to do at a cabin?

JIM: We'll go fishing, hiking, canoeing—commune with the great outdoors. You'll love it.

CHARLIE *(with obvious suspicion)*: Wait a minute . . . I want to hear more about this cabin.

JIM: It's a beautiful little rustic place with—

CHARLIE: You've seen it?

JIM: Ah . . . no. Not exactly. But I saw pictures of it on a real estate brochure.

CHARLIE: Pictures.

JIM: Pictures. You know, the things that are worth a thousand words.

CHARLIE: Then you better start talking.

JIM *(with undaunted enthusiasm, he speaks like a real estate ad)*: Like I said, it's a beautiful little cabin placed gently in a rustic setting with its own lake.

MARK: The cabin was put in a lake? What is it—a houseboat?

CHARLIE: Hush, Mark.

JIM: It has four plush bedrooms that extend from a spacious living room with romantic fireplace, a comfortably luxurious dining room and classic kitchen, mood-setting antique furniture and . . .

(As the tape fades, the lights come up onstage—a stage that looks nothing at all like JIM's description. What we see is haphazard furniture and paraphernalia indicative of days gone by. It has the look of a cabin untouched by anything human since the days

of Moses. Without missing a beat, JIM *continues his description as he enters carrying luggage. The rest of the family follow. All are looking about wide-eyed—or horrified, as the case may be.)*

JIM: . . . climaxed by a stunning view of . . . of a crystal clear lake . . . and . . . and . . .

CHARLIE: Are you sure this is it? Maybe this is the barn behind the actual cabin.

JIM: I think I'm sure. I followed the directions.

MARK *(wandering around):* Where's the TV?

(They begin spreading out to investigate. DAVID *and* BETH *wander and exit to the bedroom area.)*

CHARLIE: I wonder if this is the spacious living room or the comfortably luxurious dining room?

MARK: I hope it has a satellite dish.

*(*DAVID *and* BETH *enter again.)*

DAVID: You can forget the four plush bedrooms. There are only two and "plush" isn't the word that comes to mind.

BETH *(shivers):* There were a bunch of dead birds in there.

MARK: Maybe it's an ancient burial ground for birds. I've read about those sorts of things. I hope we're not cursed for walking in here. Maybe we should all leave.

(Everyone—but JIM*—nods in agreement and they begin to exit quietly.)*

JIM: Freeze! *(They freeze and turn around, beat.)* So it needs a little work. That's OK. It'll give us something constructive to do.

CHARLIE: If you think I'm cleaning this place up, you've got another think coming. Let the owner clean it up.

JIM: That's what I'm saying. We'll have a good time doing it.

CHARLIE: And I'd suggest that you get our rent money back. I'm not staying. *(She moves to exit, stops in her tracks, and turns to* JIM.) What did you say?

JIM *(smiling weakly):* Surprise.

CHARLIE: This is *ours?* You *bought* this?

MARK: And you pick on the clothes I wear.

JIM: It's not so bad. It just needs a little fixing up.

DAVE: A little? That's like saying the *Titanic* was *a little* fender bender.

CHARLIE: Jim . . . why? How could you?

JIM: I did it for us. For you kids. Something to be handed down through the family. A tradition. A legacy.

CHARLIE: This place doesn't look like it'll last another day let alone another generation.

JIM: We'll work on it. We'll make it into something.

MARK: What do you mean "we," kemo sabe?

(MARK *moves to exit but stops because* AUNT MATTY *enters with her nephew* SAMSON. MATTY *is quite animated in her words and behavior while* SAMSON *is inclined to stand and stare vacantly.*)

MATTY: Knock, knock. Sorry to be walking in like this, but the door was open. In fact, it's completely off the hinges. I live down the road and saw you drive past. I thought I'd give you a word of welcome . . . *(looks around at the cabin)* or encouragement.

JIM: It's nice meeting you. I'm Jim Bailey. This is my wife, Charlie, and . . .

MATTY: Charlie? That's an interesting name.

CHARLIE: It's a nickname for Charlotte.

MATTY: Ahhh, I understand. . . . My real name is Matilda. I never forgave my parents for that. That's why I go by Matty. But you don't care about that, and I didn't get the rest of your names.

BETH: Beth.

MATTY: You're a doll. This is my nephew Samson.

DAVID: She's mine and I'm David.

MATTY: Oh. I'm sorry. *(Looks to* MARK.*)*

MARK: I'm Mark.

MATTY: Well, now, don't you look sharp! The "Rambo" look is pretty hot these days. (MARK *looks at* JIM *smugly.*) I tried dressing like that one day, but the muscle shirt kept falling down to my waist. That's one of the drawbacks of getting old. *(Beat)* So you're the folks who bought Old Willard's shack. I was amazed when I heard it was sold. I couldn't imagine anyone being so . . . stupid—I mean, stupendously wise in making such a purchase. *(Looks around casually)* It's exactly as Old Willard left it . . . unfortunately.

JIM: We're going to fix it up. I think it has potential.

MATTY: Yes. Potential is a good word if you're looking for a place to keep horses. *(Beat)* I'm sorry. I didn't mean that. The thoughts sort of pop off of my tongue before I have a chance to catch them with my teeth. So what's your plan of action?

JIM: I haven't had a chance to think about it.

CHARLIE: I'd suggest dynamite.

MATTY: Oh, I'd hate to see that happen. This cabin's been here as long as I can remember. With a little care, it could be real . . . ah, it could have . . . well . . .

JIM: Potential.

MATTY: Exactly. Potential is a very good word. But I'll stop talking so much. It's been awhile since I've had new people to visit with. Samson's great fun with dominoes, but he's not much of a conversationalist as I guess you can tell. Right, Samson?

(SAMSON *gives a blank stare.*)

MATTY: But watch him on those dominoes. He cheats like a Riverboat Captain. Right, Samson?

(SAMSON *gives a blank stare.*)

MATTY: Well, I guess we should be on our way.

JIM: Maybe we can have you over for dinner when we get this place in shape.

MATTY: I could starve to death by then. How about if Samson and I give you a hand. We're good at this sort of thing. Samson used to work in a stable. *(Beat)* That didn't come out right.

JIM: I don't want to bother you.

MATTY: Don't be silly. 'Tis no bother at all. Come on . . . Let's get started. *(She moves, begins cleaning up)* This old house could be beautiful with the right people in it. *(They watch her curiously—not sure what to do.)*

JIM *(to his family):* See? It'll be great if we put ourselves into it. We've just gotta try. Are you willing to try? *(To MARK)* Mark?

MARK *(shrugs):* Sure. Maybe I'll find a satellite dish somewhere in all this junk.

(MATTY *pulls out an old radio and blows the dust off of it.*)

MATTY: It's not a satellite dish, but it might be a decent substitute. Only one station up here, Mark. WCOW. A whopping 200 watts unless someone turns a light on.

JIM: I'll bet there are all kinds of little treasures in here. What do you say? David? Beth?

DAVID: We can start cleaning out the bedrooms.

MARK: There's a surprise. (MARK *says this as he continues to play with the radio, wandering offstage to the kitchen.*)

BETH *(whispering to* DAVID*):* The dead birds.

DAVID: Maybe we better clean up outside—check the shingles, the shutters, you know. *(They exit.)*

JIM: Charlie?

CHARLIE: I know couples who have split over less than this.

JIM: But they didn't love each other as much as we do. (JIM *looks at her beseechingly.)* Come on . . . (MATTY *and* SAMSON *watch them inquisitively.)*

CHARLIE: You owe me big on this one James Michael Bailey.

JIM: I know. What do you say?

CHARLIE *(pauses, agonizes over the thought, then):* All right. We'll see what we can do.

JIM: Seal it.

CHARLIE *(embarrassed):* Jim.

JIM: If you mean it, you'll seal it.

(MATTY *and* SAMSON *watch.* CHARLIE *looks at them, they look away as if they weren't eavesdropping.* CHARLIE *goes to* JIM *and kisses him.)*

CHARLIE: There. It's sealed.

JIM *(beat, rubs hands with excitement):* This is great. This is what a family is supposed to be—joining together, hand-in-hand, unified in purpose . . .

(MARK *enters carrying an old bowl, speaking as he does.)*

MARK: Hey, look at what I found in the fridge.

(He holds it out to them. They all look and react with cringing, wincing, and general disgust. MARK *shrugs, puts a finger in it, and tastes with an expression of contemplation about its taste—as in: "Hmmm, not bad." The lights fade to blackout as we hear, taped, the voices of* BICKWOOD *and* LEWIS, *the local disc jockeys, leaving us with their voices only until the next scene.)*

BICKWOOD: And that was Merle Haggard in a trio with Willie Nelson. You're listening to Bickwood . . .

LEWIS: . . . and Lewis on . . .

BOTH IN UNISON: WCOW!

BICKWOOD: Yessirreee, Bedford Creek's only operating station.

LEWIS: We are.

BICKWOOD: Yes, indeed, we are. And coming right up, we've got the results of the Bedford Creek High School Cheerleader contest.

LEWIS: That's good news. I know a lot of folks have been waiting for this news. Spell it all out for us, Bickwood.

BICKWOOD: Well, to get a dramatic build out of this, I'll start with third place.

LEWIS: You're a tease, Bickwood.

BICKWOOD: I am. I am. But it keeps people paying attention. So here goes: it looks like third place went to Susan Belchower. I said, Susan Belchower.

LEWIS: Not bad, Susan. Of course, she would've done better if the baton hadn't slipped.

BICKWOOD: Judge Crawford'll be out of the coma in no time.

LEWIS: He will.

BICKWOOD: Of course he will. Now, the rest of the judges said it was hard picking second and first places because both Rita Harbinger and Delilah Sowmiller were so good.

LEWIS: They are, too. I've seen 'em do flips and splits that would send mere mortals screaming for deliverance.

BICKWOOD: I know it. I know it. Those girls were born without bones in their bodies. It's the only explanation I have for it. So the judges decided to give them both first place. It was the only fair thing to do.

LEWIS: I'm sure it was.

BICKWOOD: It was. Congratulations, Rita and Delilah, and all the lovely young ladies—

LEWIS: And Lester.

BICKWOOD: Yes. Him, too. Bedford Creek is proud of you. Now, on to the county competitions! *(Beat)* Lester tried out again this year?

LEWIS: Yep.

BICKWOOD: That boy ain't right. He just ain't right.

ACT ONE
Scene Two

(Night. The sound of crickets. As the lights come up, we see the Bailey family—with the exception of JIM—scattered around the stage. The stage looks a little better than when we saw it last—but not much. Off to one side, MARK has found and set up an old TV. He is sitting in front of it, watching diligently. CHARLIE is sitting on the floor in front of the couch, stretched out, eyes closed. DAVID and BETH are on the couch whispering and laughing in low tones. JIM enters.)

JIM: Quite a day, huh?

(No response)

JIM: Since we spent the entire day working on the cabin, I thought we could go hiking tomorrow.

(No response)

JIM: Or canoeing—as soon as we find the paddles. *(Beat)* And the canoe. *(Beat)* Maybe we'll just swim.

(No response)

JIM: The bedrooms are somewhat inhabitable. Charlie—you and I will take the one on the left. David and Mark can take the other one. Beth, if you don't mind, we'll put you out here on the couch.

MARK *(without taking his eyes off the TV)*: And a guard dog in the hallway.

JIM *(noticing TV)*: You got it working. *(Moves to TV)* What kind of stations are you getting?

MARK: It's a new nature format called "Snow TV."

JIM *(turning the TV off)*: That's not good for your eyes.

MARK: Hey!

JIM: OK, I've got an idea. It's something we haven't done as a family for a long time.

MARK: If he says Chinese Checkers, I'm out of here.

JIM: I want to start having family devotions together again.

MARK *(somewhat relieved)*: Boy, that was close.

JIM: Who brought a Bible? I left mine on the kitchen table at home.

(They look at each other.)

JIM: Nobody thought to bring a Bible? What kind of Christians are we that we don't take our Bibles on vacation?

MARK: Typical.

JIM: OK . . . how about favorite verses that you've memorized?

(They look at each other.)

MARK: I'll bet David could recite Song of Solomon for us. That's all he's been reading.

DAVID: Shut up, squirt. I've only read it once.

BETH: Twice.

MARK: I memorized a verse for Sunday School once.

JIM: Good for you, Mark.

MARK: "Jesus wept." *(Frowns)* But I don't remember where He did it.

JIM *(annoyed)*: Why do you do that? Why do you always have to be so glib?

MARK: I don't know. I thought I inherited it from you.

JIM (to CHARLIE): I'm going to hurt this kid.

CHARLIE: He did get it from you.

JIM: I don't care where he got it. He should get rid of it. Fine. We'll start family devotions when we get home. We'll talk, then. This is the perfect opportunity to get down to some gut-level issues. We can open up, discuss problems, get to know each other a little better. You're my family, but sometimes I believe I'm living with a bunch of strangers. It's like we don't have anything to say to each other. We don't communicate with—

DAVID: We have plenty to say, Dad.

JIM: Don't interrupt me when I'm talking, David. (Continuing) We don't communicate what's happening deep in here (gestures to heart). Now, let's go. Open up. (He stands, waiting) Come on. I've got all night if that's what it takes.

BETH (sheepishly): Excuse me, but I don't understand what the problem is. I've always had the impression that you communicate when you need to—for the important things. For instance, when David and I decided to get engaged, we came to you and talked about it in great detail.

CHARLIE: After you talked to your parents.

BETH: Yes. But I know some families who don't talk about those things at all. You guys are great. You talk about the things that count. You're a lot closer than you might think.

CHARLIE: Beth, I'm not sure you're qualified to say how close we may or may not be. Maybe when you've been around a little longer . . .

BETH: David and I have been dating for almost a year. When does the probation end?

CHARLIE: Probation? I don't know what you mean. David, do you know what she's talking about?

DAVID: I wonder what's on the TV.

MARK (jumping to turn it on): I was wondering the same thing. (He stops when JIM speaks.)

CHARLIE: Yes, I think we've done enough talking for one night. We're all very tired and obviously a little on edge.

JIM (excited that they're getting into something controversial): No, no, no . . . this is perfect. Let's go with it! Beth, you were about to say something.

BETH: David wants to go for a walk. (She stands.)

DAVID: Huh?

BETH: That walk you wanted to take—now would be a good time.

DAVID: A walk. Right. *(Struggles to stand)* I wouldn't want my body to rest any more than five minutes at a time.

(They move to exit—BETH with determination, DAVID follows and looks at JIM with bewilderment.)

JIM *(after they've gone)*: What happened? What did I miss?

CHARLIE: Everything . . . as usual. You know how sensitive she can be.

(There is a moment of frustrated silence.)

MARK *(standing)*: Well . . . since our time to have meaningful communication seems to be at a sad end, I think I'm going to walk down to Aunt Matty's and see if they want to play dominoes.

JIM: Dominoes?

MARK *(defensively)*: It's a family game.

JIM: You don't know how to play dominoes.

MARK: Samson said he'd teach me.

CHARLIE: Samson talks?

MARK: Sure.

CHARLIE *(surprised)*: I didn't hear him make a sound all day.

MARK *(shrugs)*: He doesn't talk unless he has to, I guess. *(Moves to exit)*

CHARLIE: That's the best way to be. Oh, Mark, tell Aunt Matty we'd be happy to go to church with her in the morning.

MARK: Groovy. *(MARK turns to leave, but she speaks again.)*

CHARLIE: Oh, and ask her if I could borrow her phone to make a call.

MARK: Right on.

JIM *(a significant pause after MARK's departure)*: I suppose that remark was directed at me.

CHARLIE: What remark?

JIM: You know the one . . . about not talking unless we have to.

CHARLIE *(pause)*: It's true, isn't it? Jim, I know what you're trying to do and I think it's commendable, but . . . do you have to push so hard?

JIM: I thought it would be nice to spend some time together talking. That's what families are supposed to do.

CHARLIE: But, honey, that's when there is a need to communicate. We don't have to communicate just for the sake of stirring up controversy . . . or to pry out things that are better left unsaid.

JIM: Like what? What's better left unsaid? Give me an example.

CHARLIE: Jim . . .

JIM: What is better left unsaid? What shouldn't be shared?

CHARLIE: If I thought it should be said, then I wouldn't have said it was better left unsaid.

(This sentence stops them for a moment as they check it over to be sure it makes sense. It does.)

JIM: You're thinking of something specific. Tell me what it is.

CHARLIE: Why? What would it accomplish?

JIM: It could do wonders for our marriage. Speak.

CHARLIE: We need wonders done for our marriage?

JIM: I didn't mean that. I only meant that—

CHARLIE: Are you not happy with our marriage, Jim?

JIM: Hold on . . . I didn't say that.

CHARLIE: What are you saying?

JIM: I don't know what I'm saying. I want to know what you're thinking.

CHARLIE: Why? Why are you so interested in doing that? I want to leave things just as they are. I don't want to poke and probe. I don't want any changes.

JIM: Not even for the better?

CHARLIE: What do you call "for the better"? *(Gestures to cabin)* This? Is this cabin your idea of being better? More of our hard-earned money wasted on another one of your schemes?

JIM: Money. We're back to that again.

CHARLIE: You better believe it. Why didn't you discuss buying this cabin with me before you did it?

JIM: Because you would have given me a hundred of your practical reasons why we shouldn't buy it.

CHARLIE: What's wrong with that? Heaven knows that one of us has to be practical.

JIM: Because you and I disagree on what's practical. Buying a cabin in the mountains for the family is not practical to you. But it is for me. It's very practical to me that the family should have a place of escape. With this cabin I thought we could take three or four weekends out of the year and enjoy our time away. But, no, you couldn't do that. We've been gone less than a day and you have to call Edna about that stupid Ladies Auxiliary meeting. Am I right?

CHARLIE: There were a couple of things I forgot to tell her.

JIM: There always are. Always.

CHARLIE: So I'm busy. I like being busy. I enjoy my schedule. What is it hurting? The kids are older, they don't need me at home like they used to.

JIM: You forgot somebody.

CHARLIE: Who?

JIM (*pause*): You're right. Maybe we shouldn't be having this conversation.

CHARLIE: I didn't mean that. But it's still no excuse.

JIM: Yes. You're right. It isn't. But 20 years ago *you* would have said it. You *did* say it that time you locked us in the house for the weekend. Remember? You took all the phones off of the hook and wouldn't answer the door. I was mad, but it was one of the most important weekends of our marriage. Twenty years ago you would have wanted this cabin. Those were the days when you were an impractical, impetuous, impulsive girl.

CHARLIE: And you were the very sensible, serious young man who sweated over every penny we spent. We've changed a lot since those first "I dos."

JIM: Yes, but are the changes good?

(*There is a pregnant pause as they consider this. When it's obvious there's nothing left to say . . .*)

CHARLIE: I think I'll take a stroll to Aunt Matty's. (*Sighs*) If we're keeping the cabin, I may as well get to know her better. (*She moves to exit, stops, goes back to* JIM *and kisses him, exits.*)

JIM (*after she has exited, he speaks sadly*): Tell the Ladies Auxiliary I said hello.

(*Blackout.*)

ACT ONE
Scene Three

(*Much later that night. The sound of crickets. The lights come up—dimly—on the stage. It looks the same with the exception of blankets and pillows on the couch.* BETH's *luggage sits next to it.* DAVID *and* BETH *enter from their walk. They have their arms around each other. Once inside, they turn to face each other.*)

DAVID: Good night. (*He kisses her and turns to leave. She holds onto his hand and won't let go.*)

BETH: No. Don't go yet. *(She pulls him close and embraces him.)* I won't let you go.

DAVID *(he holds her for a moment, then pulls away a little)*: You have to. It's late. We have to get up for church. *(He starts to go again.)*

BETH: No. Just hold me close. *(She embraces him tightly.)*

DAVID: If I hold you any closer, I'll be on the other side of you. *(Holds her close)* I love you, Beth.

BETH: You better. *(Hesitantly)* Do you think it's all right that I came up here with your family? I feel like I'm intruding.

DAVID: Don't be paranoid.

BETH: But your mom keeps looking at me funny . . . like she's . . . judging me or something.

DAVID: Mom has done that with every girl I've ever dated. You should have seen the looks she gave the girl I kissed in kindergarten.

BETH: Really? Why would that upset her?

DAVID: It was the teacher.

BETH: I'm being serious, David.

DAVID: Don't be serious. Forget about it.

BETH: I can't.

DAVID *(moves to her)*: Beth . . . *(Takes her hand, holds up the finger with the engagement ring on it)* See this little diamond? That's your invitation to be a part of our family. And when we get married, you're stuck with us—vacations and all. Mom'll get used to it. She really likes you. *(He embraces her.)* Really.

BETH: This is such a nice little town. Don't you think?

DAVID: Yes, it is.

BETH: Just the kind of town for some young couple in love to do something impulsive and unpredictable.

DAVID: Some young couple?

BETH: A hypothetical couple, of course.

DAVID: Of course. And what kind of impulsive and unpredictable thing do you imagine this hypothetical couple doing?

BETH: Oh . . . I suppose if they stumbled across the justice of the peace . . .

DAVID: Funny . . . I thought I saw a sign for one as we drove in.

BETH: I'll bet he's not very expensive—to do a small, quick ceremony.

DAVID: Cheaper than a big ceremony.

BETH: Just think of it, this hypothetical couple could get married . . . let's say tonight, for instance . . . and there'd be no more planning . . .

DAVID: No more cold showers.

BETH: No more decisions about wedding invitations. . .

DAVID: No more kissing good night on the porch.

BETH: No more fighting over dress colors or tuxedo styles . . .

DAVID: No more bribing a certain younger brother to get out of the house.

BETH *(enthusiastically):* We really could do it, David.

DAVID *(going along with the idea, getting equally excited):* We could leave a note for my folks, take the car, and find the justice of the peace.

BETH: We could.

DAVID *(laughs):* Wouldn't it surprise them—to wake up and find a note saying we've eloped?

BETH: We could do it, *David.*

DAVID: Yes, we could.

BETH: Then what are we waiting for?

DAVID: Nothing!

(They gather their things and exit excitedly. The stage is quiet for a moment, then . . . DAVID *and* BETH *slowly enter again, disappointed.)*

BETH: What do you mean you don't have the car keys? I thought you made copies.

DAVID: I did. But I gave them to . . . *(disheartened)* Dad.

(They put their things down.)

DAVID: It's only four months.

BETH: It was nice thinking about it.

DAVID: Yeah. Oh well . . .

BETH: I love you.

DAVID: I love you, too. *(He kisses her quickly)* Good night.

BETH: Good night.

(He drifts to exit but lingers.)

DAVID: Good night.

BETH: Good night. Don't let the bedbugs bite.

DAVID: Yeah. Right. Well . . . I love you.

BETH: I love you, too.

DAVID: Good. Well, I better go to bed now. Good night.

BETH: Good night, David.

DAVID: Good night.

JIM, CHARLIE & MARK *(shouting from offstage):* Good night already!

(Startled, he exits to the bedroom area. BETH *smiles as she drifts around the room a moment, lost in her thoughts, sits down on the couch and jumps suddenly. She pulls out a teddy bear, smiles contentedly, and pulls it close.)*

BETH: Well, Ferguson, I thought we were going to do it. Imagine that—sneaking off and getting married after all this waiting. It seems like an eternity. You know, from the first minute I met David, I knew he was the one. He was so kind and considerate . . . he's everything I've ever prayed for . . . *(Pause, smiles dreamily)* And when we get married, it'll be perfect. I just know it!

(Lights fade to blackout.)

End of Act One.

ACT TWO
Scene One

(MATTY *enters—stands on the far corner of the stage.*)

MATTY: To tell you the truth, it's a good thing David and Beth didn't try to elope. See, true romance and impulsive decisions might make for good reading, but they don't mean a thing to Desmond Wickers—he's our justice of the peace. Anybody who knows Bedford Creek would know that Desmond Wickers drinks his glass of warm milk and goes to bed promptly at nine o'clock at night and is never to be disturbed before seven in the A.M. In fact, if he falls asleep on his good ear, he might not wake up until eight. David and Beth wouldn't have known that, of course, and, well, they would have rang Desmond's bell for an eternity. They got married in the fall just as they'd originally planned. I know because they were nice enough to invite me.

(*Lights up on the stage—she slowly moves into it as she speaks. It is Christmas Eve. Late afternoon. The stage is not much different from before except for a scrawny Christmas tree that* MATTY *becomes involved in decorating.*)

MATTY (*continuing*): All of which brings us to Christmas Eve. The whole family decided to gather at the cabin and asked me and Samson to join them. A kind gesture, I thought. (*Begins speaking loudly, to* CHARLIE *offstage*) I wish Old Willard could see this. He was such a sour sort of man that this little cabin sagged under the weight of his bad disposition. With you folks, it's like it's started to stand up straight again. (*Looks at the Christmas tree*) Except for this tree.

(CHARLIE *enters carrying another box of tree decorations and puts it next to the tree. It should be fairly obvious that she is not in a particularly good mood and the tree, by her halfhearted decorating, gets the most of the abuse.*)

CHARLIE: A whole mountain of pine trees and he brings an artificial one.

MATTY (*trying to be positive*): It saves getting needles everywhere, I suppose.

CHARLIE: Jim's heart isn't in Christmas this year. I'm surprised any of us are putting in any effort. (CHARLIE *exits again.*)

MATTY: Been busy, huh?

CHARLIE (*offstage*): The usual. Mark's been real active at church and David has his job, college, and Beth. He barely has time to sleep. Beth dropped out of school to get a job but hasn't found anything.

MATTY: How do they like being married? Is it going all right?

CHARLIE: For us or for them?

MATTY: Are they still living with you?

CHARLIE: Yes.

MATTY: Then I suppose I know the answer to that question. It's tough for newlyweds to live with parents.

CHARLIE (*entering with more paraphernalia for the tree, she continues mangling it with decorations as she speaks*): You're telling me. But where else would they live? Her parents wouldn't have them. I'm happy to have them, of course, but I could strangle them both for getting married before finishing school. Especially her. She was hot to get married from the first minute they met. I'm sure the whole idea was hers.

MATTY: You might want to keep your voice down, she's in the next room.

CHARLIE: Resting. That's all she's done the past couple of weeks. I don't know what's wrong with her. Do you think I could get her to help around the house? She's always gone. She's always too busy. Do you think she's any busier than I am? Let her tell me about busy.

MATTY: She needs time to mature.

CHARLIE: So does David. It was stupid for them to get married so young. (*She exits to the kitchen.*)

MATTY (*watches her exit, pauses to look at the poor, abused tree curiously. She shivers with a sudden spell of cold and decides to try and change the subject*): I sure wish the boys had started a fire. Today would be a good day to have one. It's unusually cold even for here. Why they went fishing is beyond me. I'm sure the lake is frozen solid.

CHARLIE (*entering with more decorations, throttles the tree with tinsel*): Jim has been promising for weeks to come up and get this place ready for winter. Obviously, promises don't mean much anymore.

MATTY: Awww . . . you know how husbands can be.

CHARLIE: I thought I did.

MATTY (*tactfully*): Charlie . . . are you all right?

CHARLIE: Of course I am. Why?

MATTY (*looks at the tree, then back at* CHARLIE): If that tree were human, it could sue you for malpractice.

CHARLIE: Oh. I . . . I might be a little tense.

MATTY: Tense! You've been like a hornet in a sleeping bag.

CHARLIE (*long pause*): If I start to talk about it, I'll cry. I don't want to cry. I'll short-circuit the lights.

MATTY (*goes to her comfortingly*): Out with it, child. You can't stay like this all day.

CHARLIE: Why not? This has been going on for weeks.

MATTY: Weeks! Then you better get it out.

CHARLIE (*a thoughtful pause, moves away from her*): Something is happening to Jim and me. There's a distance between us that I've never felt before.

MATTY: That happens sometimes. Every married couple goes through phases when they feel distant. Heaven knows that Barney and I had them.

CHARLIE: No, it's more than that. We've had those phases, too. This is something different.

MATTY: What is it? Have you been fighting?

CHARLIE: No. If we fought, I might not be so afraid. It's as if he's become . . . complacent. He doesn't seem to be interested in us anymore. He lets me do what I do, and he just carries on with his life. It's almost like he doesn't care (*getting upset*), like he doesn't love me anymore.

MATTY: Oh, now I don't believe that.

CHARLIE (*controlling the tears that want to come*): You would if you knew that he's involved with another woman, Matty.

MATTY (*going to* CHARLIE, *putting her arm around her*): Oh, Charlie. What makes you think that?

CHARLIE: I told you I didn't want to cry.

MATTY: It's all right.

CHARLIE: There's this woman that he works with—Gwen is her name—and I've been told by a mutual friend that they've been seeing a lot of each other. They go to lunch together and—

MATTY: That doesn't mean anything is happening between them.

CHARLIE: One of the girls on the Policies Committee told me the other night that she saw them together at the library.

MATTY: Maybe it was a coincidence. Maybe they're both . . . studious.

CHARLIE: The library was closed.

MATTY: They didn't know the hours.

CHARLIE: They were in her Volkswagen.

MATTY: He got it confused with the night deposit box.

CHARLIE: You're not helping me any.

MATTY: No, I'm not, am I? *(Beat)* I just don't want you seeing things that aren't there. Have you talked to Jim about this?

CHARLIE: No. I don't know how to bring it up. I'm so confused. I started asking friends for advice and every one of them tells me to do something different. I've become a sniffling schizophrenic. I hate myself like this.

MATTY: Surely he notices that you've got something on your mind.

CHARLIE: No. He doesn't notice anything anymore.

MATTY: Darling, I believe you should talk to him. This isn't the way the Lord intended a marriage to be. He's your husband. You've taken vows, you've made kids, you've spent over two decades together. Talk to him.

CHARLIE: What if he says it's true?

MATTY: Then you'll know—and you'll have facts instead of gossip and speculation.

CHARLIE *(long pause)*: I don't know if those are facts I can deal with.

(Lights fade on cabin and come up on the fishing hole. We see JIM, DAVID, and MARK, sitting with fishing poles extended and lines dropped off. They are dressed warmly. MARK is wearing a heavy coat and wool cap. They sit completely still and silent, until . . .)

MARK: Are you sure this is the best part of the lake?

JIM: Pretty sure. It's so hard to see with snow covering everything.

DAVID: You know, Dad, I'm glad that you bought the cabin.

JIM: Are you? I'm glad you're glad.

DAVID: It's so good to get away and do some fishing with the guys. We couldn't do this at home.

MARK: You're right—we'd never fit around the aquarium.

DAVID *(ignoring MARK)*: You know what I mean, don't you, Dad? Doing this sort of thing satisfies a very basic masculine need. The need to get your hands dirty once, to roll up your sleeves and meet nature face-to-face.

MARK *(rolling eyes)*: Oh, brother.

DAVID: It makes me feel like . . . like a *man*.

MARK: You need all the help you can get.

DAVID: Why don't you go help Samson find some bait?

MARK: I would if I knew where he went. The movement might put some feelings back in my legs. *(Stands, moves around)*

JIM: I know what you mean, David. We haven't had much of a chance to talk—man-to-man, that is.

DAVID: Exactly. You can't talk about some things with your wife.

MARK: You can't? Why not?

JIM: Because there are some things women don't understand. It's one of the fundamental differences between men and women. Things like fishing, for instance. Good grief, could you see your mother here putting worms on a hook?

DAVID *(laughs)*: Or Beth taking the scales off of a fish?

JIM: Or cutting the heads off? There's a certain rawness to manly activity that they just can't tolerate. Women don't have the stomachs for the natural things. The sweat of the brow, the work of the hands . . .

MARK *(without missing a beat)*: . . .the changing of diapers, the cleaning of bathrooms. You're right. They couldn't possibly understand. (JIM *and* DAVID *look at him—annoyed that he's not following along.)* Never mind.

JIM: Mark, as you grow up you'll learn that men and women are different.

MARK *(flabbergasted)*: Really?

JIM: Women are dependent on men. They need us.

MARK: Well, what do you know.

DAVID: Forget it, Dad. He's clueless. *(To* MARK) Why don't you go find Samson? He might need help carrying the bait back.

MARK: You think he'll need help carrying a bunch of worms?

DAVID: Maybe he got some big ones.

MARK: Oh, I get it. You want to talk to Dad about something you don't want me to hear.

DAVID: Mark, sometimes I think you're a special kind of stupid.

MARK *(indignantly)*: Never let it be said that I couldn't take a hint.

DAVID: Take a *hike,* Mark.

MARK: I'm history. *(He moves to exit)* But if you catch anything with my pole, I get the credit. *(Exits.* JIM *and* DAVID *sit silently for a moment. Then . . .)*

DAVID: Dad, are you and Mom happy together?

JIM: What makes you ask a question like that?

DAVID: I was just wondering. You two seem so perfectly matched. Even when you fight, you know how to get it resolved.

JIM: Practice makes perfect.

DAVID: Beth and I seem to be fighting a lot lately, and none of it seems to get resolved.

JIM: You're both under a lot of pressure.

DAVID: I know. (Pause) It's ironic . . . I thought getting married would ease the pressure. It seems to have made it worse.

JIM: Waiting a little longer might have helped.

DAVID: Yeah. I suppose. (Pause) But the fact is: I don't think I would have married her at all. She's not the girl I dated, Dad. Getting married changed her. It's not what I thought it would be.

JIM: What did you expect?

DAVID: I don't know. But certainly not this. I love you and Mom, but living with you is a pain.

JIM: Thank you.

DAVID: You know how it is between Mom and Beth.

JIM: Your mother has never had to deal with another woman in the house. That takes time.

DAVID: How much time? I'm so tired of playing mediator between them that I'd like to buy them boxing gloves and let them fight to the finish.

JIM: I didn't realize it was that bad.

DAVID: You haven't been home enough to see it. And Beth . . . we don't have a physical relationship anymore. She's got a million and one excuses. She's too tired or she's not in the mood or I looked at her wrong or I said something I shouldn't or I didn't say something I should've or—

JIM: I got the idea.

DAVID: It's crazy. And she's been nagging lately—boy, oh, boy has she been nagging. She's got this idea that I'm supposed to be some sort of spiritual giant. She keeps harping at me about having devotions together and how I need to be more of a spiritual leader. I try, Dad, I really do. But between school, studying, and work—there's no time. I'm not Billy Graham, for crying out loud.

JIM: This all sounds very familiar.

DAVID: This is getting really tough, Dad. We can't hold a conversation without fighting anymore. I don't know what to do. All I keep thinking is that we've made a terrible mistake.

JIM: Do you really believe that?

DAVID: Right now? Yes. Ask me tomorrow and I won't be so sure. *(Pause)* How did you get through it, Dad? When did it stop?

JIM: Don't be so sure that it has, David.

(MARK and SAMSON enter.)

MARK: I hope you're done, because we're back. Samson couldn't find any bait. *(SAMSON leans to MARK, whispers in his ear)* Really? *(to JIM and DAVID)* Samson wants to know why we're trying to fish here. He says this is a puddle. The lake starts 10 yards over there.

(MARK points offstage. JIM and DAVID react to this as lights go down on them and come up again on the cabin. CHARLIE and MATTY are now sitting next to the tree—as decorated as this tree could ever hope to be. CHARLIE is calmer, drinking cocoa. MATTY is having hot tea.)

CHARLIE: I used to hear about situations like this and wonder how it could happen. How is it possible that even Christian marriages are falling apart? I used to judge. I used to give advice. But now it's happening to me and I feel helpless. I've read the books, watched the videos and films, sat in on the lectures . . . I've become an expert. But I think I've done it all too late.

MATTY: Funny. We never had all those things—books and films about being married, that is. We just were and worked hard to stay that way. We didn't think about it as much as folks have to now.

CHARLIE: You and your husband never had problems?

MATTY: Problems? You want a list? We had tons of them. We spent half of our lives working through them.

CHARLIE: That's a long time.

MATTY *(beat, looks at her to see if she meant to be insulting, continues)*: Doesn't seem like it now. Now . . . it seems like the blink of an eye. But, boy, did we have to work.

CHARLIE: Jim doesn't care enough to work at it anymore. *(Pause)* Last summer, when he bought this cabin, he said he was doing it to keep our family together. It made me furious. I didn't think there was anything wrong with us. Now I realize that maybe he didn't do it so we could hold on to each other. It was his way of trying to hold on to *us*.

(Noise offstage as JIM, DAVID, MARK, and SAMSON enter. CHARLIE straightens herself up. JIM wanders to the tree—looking at it with concern.)

MATTY: Did you catch anything?

MARK: Pneumonia.

MATTY: I warned you.

DAVID: We might have caught a few fish if we tried the lake. *(Moves to exit inside to bedrooms)* Beth is still sleeping?

34

CHARLIE: Of course.

DAVID: I don't know what's wrong with her. *(Exits.)*

JIM: The tree looks . . . it looks very . . . decorated.

CHARLIE: We did the best we could with what we had.

MATTY: If you folks will excuse me *(putting on coat)*, I've got to put the finishing touches on my angel costume for church tonight.

MARK: You're playing an angel?

MATTY: It was typecasting. Come on, Samson. Mark, would you like to help?

MARK: No.

MATTY: Yes you would.

MARK: No, I wouldn't.

MATTY *(very stern)*: Do it anyway.

MARK: I'd be glad to. *(Moves to exit, speaks to* SAMSON *in a deep, authoritative voice)* Let's roll, Kato. (MARK *and* SAMSON *exit.)*

MATTY: We'll be back in time for church.

CHARLIE: Thanks, Matty.

(MATTY *exits)*

JIM: We're going to church tonight?

CHARLIE: Christmas Eve service. Remember?

JIM: I don't, but that's all right. *(Begins taking off outerwear, etc.)* The place looks good, Charlie. Having Christmas here was a good idea.

CHARLIE: I'm glad you think so . . . since it was your idea.

JIM: Oh. It was, wasn't it?

CHARLIE: Jim, you know I'm not the kind of person to beat around the bush.

JIM: No, you're not. You might bludgeon the bush to death, but you don't beat around it. It's one of the things I always liked about you—you don't waste time. You get straight to the point.

CHARLIE: Are you involved with another woman?

JIM *(pause)*: Maybe you should try beating around the bush sometime. How could you ask me that question?

CHARLIE: Things have changed between us, and I've heard rumors about you and Gwen whatshername. I added two and two and came up with that question.

JIM: What kind of rumors?

CHARLIE: How many different kinds are there? I want a direct answer.

JIM: Are you sure you want to talk about this now—on Christmas Eve?

CHARLIE: Yes. *(Beat)* No. *(Closes eyes to compose herself)* Wait. I'm afraid.

JIM: Afraid?

CHARLIE: I've spent weeks playing out this scene in my mind and now that I'm here, I'm afraid that it won't end the way I want it to.

JIM: How do you want it to end, Charlie?

CHARLIE: You take me in your arms and tell me everything's OK and we'll go on living as we have for over 20 years.

(CHARLIE looks at him—as if expecting JIM to play out the scene that way. He doesn't move. He stands silently.)

CHARLIE: That's not how this scene is going to end, is it?

JIM: No, Charlie. Not this time.

CHARLIE *(toughening up):* Then you better answer the question.

JIM: It doesn't have a simple answer.

CHARLIE: That means "yes."

JIM: No, it doesn't. If you're asking me to say I'm involved with Gwen—yes, I am. If you're asking me to say I've committed adultery—no, I haven't. Gwen and I have become good friends. We talk, we share mutual interests, we enjoy each other's company. It's like you and your Ladies Auxiliary group.

CHARLIE: You're buddies, right? That's what I'm supposed to believe? You're a couple of pals who hang out together.

JIM: Basically, that's it.

CHARLIE: Don't insult my intelligence.

JIM: I'm not. It's the truth.

CHARLIE: Do you love her?

JIM: I care for her.

CHARLIE: Do you love her, Jim?

JIM: Not like you're thinking of it.

CHARLIE: Could you love her?

JIM: That's not a fair question.

CHARLIE: Don't expect me to be fair, Jim. Not now. Are you attracted to her?

JIM: Good grief, Charlie, what do you want to know? What are you digging for? Isn't it enough that I've told you what I have? *(Groans)* Why women do that I'll never know. You dig for the guilt no matter how you can find it. If you can't catch the man in the action then you nail him for the attitude. Nothing has happened between me and Gwen. Not even a hug.

CHARLIE *(calmly)*: I believe you. Now answer the question. Are you attracted to her?

JIM: Of course I am. I wouldn't be human if I wasn't attracted to her. Are you satisfied? Having admitted that is the same as if I'd done it, right?

CHARLIE: The Bible hints at that, I think.

JIM: Oh, no you don't. If you're going to use the Bible as a weapon, I'm leaving.

CHARLIE: I'm just trying to understand! How has this happened to us? Why are you interested in her?

JIM: Because she's having a hard time right now and she needs someone. Helping others—that's a scriptural principle, isn't it?

CHARLIE: If I can't use the Bible, you can't either. You're telling me that she needs you.

JIM: Yes, she needs me. It's nice to be needed for once.

CHARLIE: What about me? I need you.

JIM: No, you don't. You haven't needed me for ages. You are totally in control—your life, your habits, your emotions. You are a . . . fortress. I used to love the security of that. But now it feels like a prison. I feel locked in.

CHARLIE: Why haven't you told me all this before?

JIM: I have. You weren't listening.

CHARLIE: So what's the answer? Do you want me to change? Tell me how you would like me to change.

JIM: I don't know. I can't answer that right now.

CHARLIE: Why not? Obviously you've been thinking a lot about it.

JIM: Because to ask you to change means that I have to be willing to change. I don't know if I want to do that now.

CHARLIE: What are we supposed to do?

JIM: I don't know. *(Pause)* I don't know. Charlie, if I could end the scene the way you want and take you in my arms and whisper that everything will be OK, I would. But I can't.

CHARLIE: Then what do you want?

JIM *(thoughtful pause)*: I want to go in, get ready for church, and make the most of this holiday with my family. *(Beat)* And pray the rest of the answers will show up in my Christmas stocking tomorrow morning. *(He moves to exit inside.)*

CHARLIE: Jim. *(He turns to her.)* Do you love me?

JIM: You should know the answer to that. *(He exits.)*

CHARLIE *(after he leaves)*: I should. But I don't.

(She sits silently for a moment, lost in her thoughts. MARK enters carrying Christmas gifts. He dumps them next to the tree.)

MARK: I think Aunt Matty got carried away. *(As he speaks, he takes off his hat and coat to reveal spiked hair with purple streak and a moderately "punk/new wave" outfit.)* She and Samson will be up in a minute with more. You should see her angel outfit. It's a riot. *(Beat)* You know, she says this is the best Christmas she's had in years. *(Pauses, looks at CHARLIE)* Why do I get the feeling that she's the only one who feels that way? *(CHARLIE continues to remain lost in her thoughts.)* Yeah, that's what I think, too.

CHARLIE *(realizing that someone is talking)*: I'm sorry, were you talking to me?

MARK *(looks around)*: I hope so.

CHARLIE *(looking at MARK's hair)*: Why did you dye your hair purple?

MARK: Because I ran out of blue.

CHARLIE: I think I liked your "Rancho" outfit better.

MARK: "Rambo." And it was boring.

CHARLIE: You look like somebody's nightmare.

MARK: Thank you.

(Silence ensues as CHARLIE loses herself in her thoughts again. MARK watches her curiously.)

MARK: Mom.

CHARLIE *(she returns, sees the gifts under the tree)*: Where did all these gifts come from?

MARK *(reacts with bemusement)*: Mom, are you all right?

CHARLIE: I'm fine. Where did these gifts come from?

MARK: I brought them in. Didn't you see me?

CHARLIE *(pauses)*: Yes. Of course I did.

MARK: Mom, what's wrong?

CHARLIE: Nothing's wrong.

MARK: Something's wrong. The last time you acted like this was when Grandpa was found bowling in his underwear. He hasn't done anything else, has he?

CHARLIE: Grandpa? No. He's still at the convalescent center. Why—have you heard something about him?

MARK: Mom, check your circuits. You're not running full capacity with me.

CHARLIE: What does that mean?

MARK (*sits down next to her*): What's troubling you, my child? Tell Uncle Mark all about it.

CHARLIE: It's not something I can talk about.

MARK: Oh. (*Pause*) Is there something I can do?

CHARLIE: Pray. Pray real hard.

MARK: I can do that. Is there anything else?

CHARLIE: Would you give me a hug?

MARK: I can do that, too. (*He hugs her, she breaks down and begins to cry, burying her face in his shoulder.*) It'll be all right, Mom. Whatever it is, we'll make it better.

(*The lights fade to blackout as the voices of* BICKWOOD *and* LEWIS *can be heard, taped, behind them, we can hear a frightening organ rendition of "Joy to the World."*)

BICKWOOD: I'm Bickwood.

LEWIS: I'm Lewis, and we're broadcasting live from our own Fellowship Community Church right here in Bedford Creek.

BICKWOOD: We certainly are.

LEWIS: Absolutely live for the Christmas Eve service here at Fellowship—no tapes, no gimmicks, as I'm sure you can hear from the fine organ playing by Eustice MacKenzie. Say hello, Eustice.

(*The organ swells in response.*)

BICKWOOD: You play it, Eustice!

LEWIS: She's the Liberace of church organists.

BICKWOOD: She is.

LEWIS: She most certainly is, and we're live this Christmas Eve and looking forward to a fine little Nativity pageant from the Fellowship drama group.

BICKWOOD: Featuring the multitalented Henry Bickwood as the sheep on the far left.

LEWIS: That's your son.

BICKWOOD: My son. Well, we see Pastor Cropfitz moving to the podium to lead in the opening song so we'll just shut up.

LEWIS: We will.

BICKWOOD: We better. He hates competition.

(The congregation can be heard singing "Joy to the World" as the tape fades into the next scene.)

ACT TWO
Scene Two

(Later that night. Lights up on the stage. In spite of itself, it has a nice, warm, Christmassy look and feel to it. JIM, CHARLIE, MARK, DAVID, BETH, SAMSON, *and* MATTY *in her angel outfit under her coat, enter—just arriving from church—begin taking off outerwear.* BETH *sits down, she looks tired.* DAVID *sits next to her.* MATTY *takes off her coat to reveal the angel outfit. Everyone stares as her silently.)*

MATTY: What's everybody looking at? Haven't you seen an angel before?

MARK: You look more like a tooth fairy.

MATTY: Mind your manners, smart kid. I have friends in high places.

JIM *(by the tree):* This tree isn't so bad with all the presents underneath.

CHARLIE: What do you think is holding the thing up?

MARK: Presents! Let's open some presents.

CHARLIE: You have to wait until tomorrow morning.

MARK: Why?

CHARLIE: Because it's . . . tradition. We don't open our presents until Christmas morning. You know that.

MARK: Maybe it's time to change the tradition.

CHARLIE: Please. I've had enough changes for one Christmas.

MATTY: How about some eggnog? That's a good tradition. *(She moves to exit.)*

CHARLIE: Let me help, Matty. *(Begins to follow)*

JIM: Are you sure you shouldn't be serving angel food cake?

(He laughs—no one else does. Suddenly, SAMSON *lets out a brief burst of laughter, then stops himself self-consciously.* CHARLIE *rolls her eyes and exits.)*

MATTY: So how many glasses are we pouring?

BETH: Not for me. I don't feel very good.

DAVID: Still? Beth, you're going to a doctor as soon as we get home.

BETH: I'll be OK. It comes and goes.

MATTY: Everyone but Beth. Eggnog coming right up. *(Exits.)*

JIM *(calling after her):* That was a good service tonight, Matty. You have a nice church.

DAVID: Interesting topic the pastor preached about . . . Christmas and the need for family unity.

BETH: Very timely, I thought.

MARK: I enjoyed the reenactment of the Nativity scene. I've never seen a church use a real cow in the sanctuary before.

JIM: They shouldn't have fed her before the service, though.

(CHARLIE enters with paper cups filled with eggnog and begins handing them out.)

CHARLIE: Home-made eggnog. Matty made it herself. *(MATTY enters with more to hand out.)*

MATTY: I couldn't imagine Christmas without it. It's been a tradition in my family since the beginning of time. I'll bet even Adam and Eve had eggnog on Christmas Eve.

MARK: Apple cider.

JIM: You know what? I want to make a toast.

BETH: So do I.

JIM *(surprised):* You do? Well, please, ladies first.

BETH: I just want to make a toast to this family because I think you're . . . you're wonderful. I know it's been difficult for all of us the past few months but . . . I love you all very much and I'm proud to have my baby grow up in such a family.

MATTY: That's sweet.

JIM: OK, now for my toast . . .

(He raises his glass and suddenly, in a corporate reaction, everyone turns to BETH and says . . .)

EVERYONE: Baby!

DAVID: Did you say "baby"?

BETH (nods proudly): Yes. I'm pregnant.

DAVID: But . . . but how?

(Everyone deadpans a look at DAVID.)

MARK: Now *that's* a special kind of stupid.

DAVID: Beth, tell me you're joking.

BETH (looks surprised at DAVID): I thought you'd be happy.

DAVID: Happy! Happy? (Not happy) I am! It's just that . . . we can't . . . I mean . . . pregnant? (Groans, moves to exit inside) I think I better lay down. (He exits.)

BETH: David? (Moves to follow) David! (She exits.)

MARK: The plot begins to thicken.

(CHARLIE rubs her brow, shaking her head in disbelief as attention goes back to JIM.)

MATTY: You were saying?

JIM (raising glass hesitantly): I . . . I think this whole holiday can be . . . (clears his throat) the start of something new and life-changing. And now this new bit of news. I'm going to be a grandfather. It couldn't be any more complete. So, I . . . I wanted to raise a toast to the one thing that has helped bring this all about. To this . . . cabin. Already it's becoming a family tradition.

CHARLIE (shocked): You're toasting this *cabin*?

JIM: Yes. You don't want to toast the cabin?

CHARLIE: Yes I'd like to toast this cabin—with a flamethrower! (She storms off to inside.)

JIM: Charlie? (To the remaining people) What did I say?

MATTY (moving to inside to aid CHARLIE): I think you better work on your timing, Jim. (Exits.)

JIM (moving to follow): What is it? What have I said? (Exits, leaving MARK and SAMSON—who look blankly at each other.)

MARK (lifts cup dryly to SAMSON): Merry Christmas.

(SAMSON grunts as he lifts his cup.)

(Lights fade to blackout.)

End of Act Two.

ACT THREE
Scene One

(Spring, around Easter. Early afternoon. MATTY enters and stands to one side of the stage. She is dressed in a referee's uniform [black and white shirt] with a whistle strung around her neck. As she speaks, the lights come up and the Baileys enter silently with plates of food. There is a weighted silence, a somberness between them. They are dressed as if they've all been working on the cabin—which they have. BETH, who is now five months pregnant, struggles with sitting down. MARK, even though working, should be dressed very stylish [aka Southern California fashionable]. His hairstyle should reflect a similar fashion [no more punk/new wave]. The stage looks different—almost empty in its cleanliness, barren of any "homey" touches.)

MATTY: Hi. I'm back again to explain a few things—though this is gonna be tough. You see, after Christmas, Samson and I seemed to lose touch with the Baileys. Or they lost touch with us. Hard to explain, really, because all of a sudden the letters stopped coming and the one or two attempts at calling were very . . . brief. "Too busy" is what I got. Considering where we left off last Christmas, I wasn't surprised. Families always seem to throw the walls up to outsiders when they have trouble. Rather than reach out for help, they just put on a good face, make excuses, and pretend like everything's all right. Well, a couple of months of this and then an early spring sneaked up on us just like Wilmer down at the drugstore said it would. I don't know how Wilmer knows these things, but he can always tell what the weather's going to do. The man's a walking almanac. With the thaw, I got busy with my usual springtime activities—that's why I'm dressed like this, I coach the girls' softball team and let me tell you, they can whup the britches off of just about any boys' team they've played. It isn't very ladylike, but it's sure satisfying. What was I saying? Oh yeah, Jim started coming around the cabin more and more. Not that he'd talk much—he was politely distant. But he'd work on that cabin like it was the only thing he had and, sure enough, it started to shape up. I guess it was around Easter *(she turns to look at the Baileys on stage)* —yes, Easter it was—they all suddenly showed up. Things were different . . . but not necessarily better.

(MATTY exits. The Baileys continue to eat in their brooding silence.)

DAVID: So . . . what now?

JIM: Just a few more things, and then we'll call it a day.

MARK: Boy, Dad, holidays don't get much better than this. Easter cleaning up the cabin. Maybe for Memorial Day I'll get a root canal.

JIM: It needs to be done, and this is the only time to do it. Deal with it. (JIM *pulls out a small booklet*) Whose turn is it for devotions? (*Looks around, no one responds*) Come on, I did it yesterday, which means . . .

MARK: It's me. (JIM *tosses him the booklet. He opens it, searches for the correct page.*) What's today?

JIM: Saturday.

MARK: Right. (*Glances at the page*) Oh, goodie. (*Begins reading without expression or emotion*) Ephesians chapter 5, "Wives, submit to your husbands as to the Lord. For the husband is head of the wife as also Christ is head of the church . . ."

DAVID: Amen. (BETH *looks at* DAVID *annoyed.*)

MARK: "Husbands, love your wives just as Christ loved the church and gave himself up for it. So husbands ought to love their own wives as their own bodies."

CHARLIE: Such is the distance between the truth of scripture and reality.

MARK: "Nevertheless, let each one of you in particular love his own wife as himself, and let the wife see that she respects her husband." (MARK *tosses the booklet back to* JIM) Batteries not included. Void where prohibited. Some assembly required.

JIM: You could have done it with a little more enthusiasm.

MARK: We all could. Look, guys, serious biz here . . . I mean, maybe it's just me, but I think we need to clear the air.

DAVID: Open a window.

MARK: You know what I'm talking about. Things just aren't right.

JIM (*stands*): I think we should get back to work. Let's get these dishes to the kitchen.

(*Everyone begins to do that.* MARK *watches them helplessly.*)

MARK: Maybe it *is* just me.

(MATTY *and* SAMSON *enter.* MATTY *is dressed as she was at the beginning of the act.* SAMSON *is dressed as he always is.*)

MATTY: Hellooo, Bailey family! I was on my way to the ball game when I saw your car. Welcome back. What are you busy beavers up to?

JIM: Just working on the cabin.

CHARLIE (*to* MATTY): Are you playing today or refereeing?

MATTY: Coach. They won't let me play.

MARK: Why not?

MATTY: I wear them out. They can't keep up with me. (To MARK) I've got a fastball that'll curl the hair in your nose.

MARK: I'd like to see it sometime.

JIM (to group): OK, gang, let's get back to work. Sorry, Matty, we have a lot to do.

(General moans.)

BETH: I can't. I don't feel very good.

DAVID (sarcastically): Now there's something new.

MATTY: You're still sick?

DAVID: She's been sick every day since Christmas. It's turning out to be a long nine months.

MATTY: The first few months are the worst. Maybe you should rest for a while.

JIM: Fine. You rest, Beth. Gang, let's go.

CHARLIE: I think we should call it quits for the day, Jim. We've done a lot today. Besides, I'm getting a headache.

JIM: Oh, I get it. Sure. Do what you want—I need to get back to work on the new bathroom.

MATTY: A new bathroom? How is it new?

JIM: It'll be inside the cabin instead of up on the hill. Anyone not too busy with other things can help me there.

(Everyone looks away.)

JIM: Mark?

MARK: And mess up my threads? Come on, Dad, be reasonable.

JIM (moves to exit): I think I liked your "punk" phase better—at least then you didn't worry about getting your clothes dirty . . . they already were. (Exits.)

MARK: I'm graduating in a couple of months. I can't stay a child all my life.

CHARLIE: Why not? You're your father's son.

JIM (from offstage): I heard that!

MARK: I need to go to the post office to mail in some college applications.

MATTY: Oh, that's right—you're going to be a college boy this fall.

MARK: College man, Aunt Matty. (He moves to exit, chest thrust forward and proudly inflated, voice substantially deeper and "macho.") College man. You wanna come with me, Samson?

(SAMSON *nods, follows, imitates* MARK's *walk as he does. They exit.*)

BETH (*cuddles up to* DAVID *affectionately*): Let's go for a walk, David. It's a beautiful spring day and—

DAVID (*moves away from her*): Maybe later. I think I'll help Dad with the bathroom. (*He exits.*)

BETH (*obviously hurt*): Sure. Later. (*Beat*) So much for the joys of wedded bliss.

MATTY (*trying to comfort*): The bathroom needs work, Beth.

BETH: That's not the only thing.

MATTY: Really?

CHARLIE: Now, Beth, you need to be careful with statements like that. You're giving Aunt Matty the wrong impression.

BETH: No, I think Aunt Matty will get a very accurate impression.

CHARLIE: Beth, don't get started. Why don't you go take a nap?

BETH: A nap? I'm not a child, and I don't need a nap. I need my husband, and right now it feels like he's a million miles away.

MATTY: Aw, honey, you're just sensitive because you're pregnant. I'm sure he—

BETH: My pregnancy has nothing to do with it. My marriage was in trouble before I got pregnant.

(*We begin to hear pounding from the back—pipes and such—inconsistent yet extremely annoying.*)

CHARLIE: How can you say that?

BETH: It's true. I won't ignore it anymore.

CHARLIE: Do you think it's been easy on David? He's tired, he's under a lot of pressure (*an obvious jab*)—it's not easy exhausting yourself to support a pregnant wife.

BETH: You say that as if it's my fault.

CHARLIE: Well?

BETH: It took the two of us to make me this way.

CHARLIE: At least you could work harder to be less of a . . . a burden.

BETH: Oh, that's what I've become. A burden?

CHARLIE: I didn't mean burden, I meant . . . responsibility.

BETH: No. You were right the first time. That's the way it's been. I feel like I've become nothing more than a responsibility to David. He tolerates me because he thinks he has to. I don't want toleration, I married David for love.

CHARLIE (*laughs resentfully*): What do you think you know about love? What do either of you know?

BETH: What am I supposed to know? Why don't you explain it to me. Help me, Charlie. He's your son. Tell me what to do. I'm losing him just like you're losing Jim.

(*Stunned silence.*)

CHARLIE: I resent that remark.

BETH: You know it's true. We both have husbands who are growing more distant all the time. Maybe we can both figure out how to bring them back—you and me. Together.

CHARLIE: I don't know what you're talking about.

BETH: You know. You know. You just won't say it. I don't know why you won't open up to me. I don't know what I've done to make you hate me so much. I've tried to—to get close to you. But you keep shutting me out. You've kept us perfect strangers.

MATTY: Calm down, Beth, don't get yourself worked up. The baby.

BETH (*upset, puts hands over her ears*): I wish they would stop pounding.

CHARLIE: You want my advice, Beth? Stop being so emotional. It turns David off. It turns us all off.

BETH: That's it? That's your advice? Is that how I should get David back? Stop being so emotional. But it hasn't worked for you and Jim—has it? Nothing has. Just because he stopped seeing that woman, you thought it would be all right. But it's just as bad as it was before.

CHARLIE: That's none of your business! You have no right bringing that up. You tend to your husband, and I'll tend to mine.

BETH: But I don't know how! Don't you understand? I don't know how. (*She exits tearfully to the bedroom.*)

MATTY: It's not healthy for her to get so upset.

CHARLIE (*rubs temples*): You're telling me. (*Shouts to the back*) Stop that pounding back there! You're driving us crazy!

(*The pounding stops.*)

MATTY: Charlie . . . is there something going on that we should talk about? Maybe it's none of my business, but—

CHARLIE: It's nobody's business but mine and Jim's. She had no right saying what she did.

MATTY: OK. I don't want to pry.

CHARLIE: Then don't.

(The abruptness of this statement stops them both.)

MATTY: Well . . . I should be going then. I'm sorry if I intruded. *(She moves to exit as the pounding begins again.)*

CHARLIE: Wait . . . (MATTY *stops.)* I'm sorry. I didn't mean that.

MATTY: I don't ever want you to think that I'm trying to stick my nose in your business. I only want to help if I can.

CHARLIE: I know. *(Pauses, gets agitated again)* Do you see what's happened? Do you see how cruel I've become? *(Pauses, speaks more softly)* What Beth said was true. I didn't realize she knew what was happening.

MATTY: Kids pick up on a lot more than we like to think.

CHARLIE *(pause):* Jim and I made an even trade. He stopped seeing his friend, and I dropped out of all my activities.

MATTY: And?

CHARLIE: And I thought it would make everything better.

MATTY: Did it?

CHARLIE: For a little while I thought it did. I really believed it would work. But something was— is—still missing. I get angry over the smallest things now and . . . I haven't been happy at all. In a lot of ways, it's worse than it was before. *(Pause)* I gave up everything and do you know what he does? He comes up to work on this cabin. At least with that Gwen I knew what the attraction was. But *this*—he's obsessed with it! *(Beat)* I resent it. I resent giving up my life, the things I enjoy the most, only to have him replace it with this trash heap. *(Screams at the back)* Stop pounding! I can't stand the pounding anymore!

(The pounding stops.)

CHARLIE: Now I don't care anymore, Matty. It doesn't matter to me what happens. I just want an end to this.

MATTY: Charlie, maybe these are symptoms of something deeper. Maybe you're missing the heart of the problem—something spiritual, something the Lord is trying to tell you. Y'know, there was a time when Barney and I had a spell—

(JIM and DAVID enter.)

JIM: What's all the screaming about?

CHARLIE: What do you expect us to do with all that pounding back there? Let me take a hammer to your pipes and see how you like it.

DAVID: Where's Beth?

CHARLIE: She's in her room. And now I have a headache.

DAVID: Why is she in bed? Is she sick again?

CHARLIE: You'll have to ask her.

DAVID: You two have been arguing again, right? *(Groans)* What now? Can't you two be left alone for a minute without fighting about something? (DAVID *exits to bedroom.)*

JIM: Will someone explain to me what's going on? *(To* MATTY*)* Matty? You seem coherent today. What's happening here?

CHARLIE: Go ahead. Ask Matty. Don't ask me.

JIM: I'm asking you. What's the problem here?

CHARLIE: Figure it out.

JIM *(to* MATTY*)*: Are these symptoms of mid-life crisis or what?

MATTY: I wouldn't know. I haven't hit mid-life yet.

CHARLIE: If you cared as much about us as you do this cabin, you'd know what's going on.

JIM: What does this cabin have to do with anything? Why are you always picking on this cabin? You want me to give this up, too?

CHARLIE: Too! What else have you given up?

JIM: I've given up . . . a few things.

CHARLIE: What? Spell it out for me, Jim. What have you given up?

JIM: I don't think this is the place to—

CHARLIE: This is a great place. Go ahead. Say what it was you gave up.

JIM: Charlie, stop it.

CHARLIE: I'll give you her first initial. It was Gwen. Right?

JIM: OK. Fine. If that's how you want to play it. Yes. I gave up Gwen—a good friend. What more do you want, Charlie?

CHARLIE: You didn't give up Gwen—she went back to her husband. *(Points accusingly)* Aha—see, you didn't know I knew that! You thought you were being Mr. Noble and gave her up willingly. I knew better.

JIM: Who do you think convinced her to get back with her husband? I did.

CHARLIE: Of course you did. You're the great fixer-upper. You fix cabins, you fix other people's marriages—

JIM: Charlie, what is your problem? I gave her up. It's done.

(MARK *and* SAMSON *enter in the midst of this.* MARK *surveys the scene.*)

CHARLIE: It's not done because I gave up everything else.

JIM: Ladies Auxiliary. Now there's a sacrifice.

MARK: We'll come back later. *(Turns to leave again.)*

CHARLIE: No! You stay right where you are, young man. I want you to see this.

JIM: Why drag him into this?

CHARLIE: I want him to see his true mother and father.

MARK: You mean I'm adopted?

CHARLIE: Always a joke, always a witty remark. Is that how you deal with it all—make a smart remark and run off?

MARK: Why stay home? It's safer to have a strong exit line and get off the stage. I tried to talk about it.

JIM: Leave him out of this. It's our problem and we'll deal with it.

CHARLIE: Deal with it? When will we deal with it? After you've finished renovating the cabin?

(DAVID *and* BETH *enter. All the dialogue begins to mix and build to a harsh intensity.*)

JIM: The cabin again. You keep harping on this cabin. You've never forgiven me for not getting your permission to buy it.

DAVID: I want you to apologize for whatever it was you said.

CHARLIE: That has nothing to do with anything. You should have checked with me first but that's insignificant now.

BETH: There's nothing to apologize for. I won't do it. I need to lay down.

JIM: Then why do you keep bringing it up? The problem isn't in this cabin, it's in you and me!

DAVID: Apologize! As your husband, I'm telling you to do it. You're supposed to submit to me.

MARK *(to* SAMSON*)*: Are we here for a reason?

(SAMSON *shrugs.*)

BETH: When you start behaving like a husband, I might start submitting to you. Please, David, I don't feel well.

CHARLIE: You better believe there's a problem. It's about time you acknowledged it.

(At this point, MATTY has taken her whistle in hand and now blows it loudly. Everyone stops and looks at her.)

MATTY: All right, all right! Everyone off the ice. We'll have a face-off in the center.

BETH: It hurts, David. I better lay down. I need to lay down.

(Clutching her stomach, BETH rushes offstage to the bedroom area.)

DAVID *(as authoritative as he can sound, exits as he speaks)*: Beth, don't you dare leave this room.

MARK: That's telling her.

MATTY: There are good, productive ways to fight to get things resolved. This is not one of those ways.

(DAVID enters again—panicked. Everyone reacts almost simultaneously as the scene moves.)

DAVID: Mom, Matty—come quick. There's something wrong with Beth. She's . . . she's . . . (MATTY *and* CHARLIE *rush past him to interior as he speaks*) Dad, we've got to get her to a hospital. (MARK *moves on his line as* DAVID *turns and goes back into the bedroom.*)

MARK: I'll get the car. *(He exits to exterior.)*

JIM: What is it? What's wrong?

(MATTY enters—moves to phone as she speaks to anyone and no one in particular.)

MATTY: Hospital's too far. I'll call Doc Fisher. He can be here in a minute. (*Picks up phone and dials.* JIM *moves to* MATTY.)

JIM: What is it, Matty? What's happened?

MATTY: I think she's lost the baby.

(Blackout.)

ACT THREE
Scene Two

(Before the lights come up, we hear the ticking of an old clock. It is later. Lights up on the stage. Everyone—except MATTY and BETH—is sitting or standing anxiously—flipping through magazines, pacing, looking at the time, etc.—DAVID stands off to one side, lost in his own thoughts.)

MARK: Maybe I should turn on the radio.

CHARLIE: Maybe you should. A little music might be—

DAVID *(obviously irritated)*: No. No music. Couldn't we just wait quietly for once?

MARK: Sure, David. *(Stands, moves to exit)* I think I'll wait outside. Come on, Samson.

(SAMSON *nods, stands, hesitantly goes to* DAVID—*gently pats his shoulder sympathetically—then follows* MARK *out.*)

DAVID (*after they exit*): What's taking so long?

CHARLIE: I'm sure the doctor is doing the best he can. You wouldn't want him to rush, would you?

DAVID: No. No, I guess not. I just wish I knew what was happening in there.

CHARLIE: I'll go see. (*She exits interior. After a moment,* JIM *moves to* DAVID.)

JIM: Son . . . try to relax. It'll be all right.

DAVID: I want to believe that, Dad. (*Pauses, speaks as if to himself*) If anything happens, I'll—I'll never forgive myself.

JIM: Don't talk like that. It's not your fault.

DAVID: Yes it is. Dad, she's my wife. I'm supposed to be responsible for her. I've really blown it.

JIM: Don't be so hard on yourself.

DAVID: Why not?

JIM: Because . . . (*at a loss for words*)

DAVID: You'd feel the same.

JIM: I do feel the same.

DAVID (*after a moment*): Dad, I feel like I've been sleeping, and I'm finally waking up. Where have I been? What have I been doing in my marriage? (*Agonizing*) O God, this has to turn out all right. I'd give anything to undo the last few months—anything to make it better. I've been so wrong.

JIM: I know what you mean, son. I know what you mean.

(JIM *and* DAVID *embrace.*)

CHARLIE: Matty will be right out. (*After a moment of silence as she moves across the room*) This is the bottom, isn't it? We've gone as low as we can. No words. No comfort. The bottom.

JIM: At least at the bottom we can't argue about where we are.

(MATTY *enters. Speaks to* DAVID.)

MATTY: Doc wants you to come in.

(MARK *and* SAMSON *enter as* DAVID *exits.*)

MARK: What's going on? What—?

CHARLIE: Beth is all right?

MATTY: Yes, she'll be fine. *(Pause)* She miscarried.

(Stunned pause, then reactions of sadness.)

MATTY: I'm very sorry. Doc did everything he could. Now she needs to rest. *(To MARK)* Mark, will you drive me down to the drugstore? I need to get some prescriptions for her.

MARK: Sure. Anything.

(MARK and SAMSON exit. MATTY starts to follow but pauses.)

MATTY: It wasn't anybody's fault. These things happen. It's important you know that.

JIM: Is there anything we can do?

MATTY: Pray. Pray together real hard. The next few days are going to be very difficult for Beth . . . for all of you. *(She exits as JIM and CHARLIE look at each other uneasily.)*

JIM *(after a long pause):* Can we do that?

CHARLIE: What—pray? I don't know. We should.

JIM: We need to. Beth needs us to.

(They look at each other sadly for a moment.)

CHARLIE: I never hated her, Jim. I know everyone thinks so—but I never did.

JIM: We need to pray together, Charlie.

CHARLIE: I'm not sure how anymore. We haven't prayed together in a long time. *(Moves away, heartfelt agony in her voice)* Oh, Jim, this is horrible. You're my husband and I can't even pray with you. Is this what God has to resort to to make us realize what kind of people we are?

JIM: Maybe if we'd prayed together more, we wouldn't be where we are.

CHARLIE: Maybe?

JIM: Charlie . . . I think it's time to get this settled.

CHARLIE *(pauses, nods):* Yes . . . But I don't know where to start.

JIM *(hesitates, considers it):* Then I'll start. *(Pauses, speaks slowly, his words measured at first and then more intense as he continues.)* Earlier, when Mark recited those scripture verses—you know what I kept thinking to myself? I kept thinking that I needed to get back to work on the bathroom. I didn't want to hear them. But when I got back there, I kept thinking about those verses, so I started pounding harder to get them out of my mind, and I felt very guilty. So I pounded even harder to make it go away—like I've tried to use the cabin to make all the problems go away. And I looked at David and thought what a terrible example I've been to him in all this. It's like his marriage has been a reflection of ours. So he said, "Dad, why are you pounding so hard?" And I said, "It's therapeutic!" And so he started pounding harder too. And there we were, the two of us, beating those pipes within an inch of their lives. Then you screamed at us to stop and when I came in, there you were—completely out of control. I've never seen you out of control, Charlie. Never. And those verses—those confounded verses—kept coming back to my mind.

CHARLIE: Jim, I don't know what all of this has to do with—

JIM: In the end, Charlie, all I could think to do is ask for your forgiveness—for not being your husband these past few months—for making bargains with you instead of making sacrifices—for not loving you as Christ loves the church. *(Pauses)* Can you—will you—forgive me?

CHARLIE *(she is surprised by this but tries to cover it, thinks carefully before responding)*: We've spent the past six months tying ourselves up into emotional knots—knots so tight I thought I'd strangle to death.

JIM: I know.

CHARLIE: Untying them all won't be so easy.

JIM: No, it won't. But if we're both willing to try—to work at those knots—then there's no reason we can't do it. One by one, Charlie. We can get back to where we can breathe again—even love again. If we're both willing.

CHARLIE *(echoing his words thoughtfully but noncommitally)*: If we're both willing.

JIM *(pause, speaks with resolve)*: I am willing. Are you?

CHARLIE *(there is a long silence that reflects inner turmoil)*: I keep thinking about the last time we talked about being willing. It was when we got married. I said, "I will." *(Another thoughtful pause)* I've regretted that commitment once or twice over the past few months, Jim. There were times when I wished to God I never made it.

JIM: I've had a few of those moments myself.

CHARLIE: It's going to take some time for the feelings to come back, Jim. *(Slowly, hesitantly, knowing its the right thing to say)* But . . . a commitment I made and a commitment I'll keep.

JIM: Is that a "yes"?

CHARLIE *(sighs)*: It is. *(Breathes in deeply as if mustering her courage to give in, speaks with resolve but without excitement)* Whatever it takes, Jim—I'll do. We'll talk, we'll get counseling . . . we'll fix the bathrooms in 10 cabins if we have to. By the grace of God, we'll try to make it work again.

JIM: Then you'll forgive me?

CHARLIE: Yes. Will you forgive me?

JIM: Yes.

(She takes a step toward him, awkwardly extends her hand a short way to him. He responds, stepping toward her, taking her hand, then slowly embracing her.)

JIM: Remember when you said you wanted the scene to end with me holding you and telling you it'll be all right?

CHARLIE: Yes.

JIM: Charlie . . . it'll be all right. It won't be easy—but it'll be all right.

(They embrace again.)

CHARLIE: Now we can pray for Beth.

JIM: We can.

CHARLIE: And we'll pray for us, too.

*(They exit together as lights fade to blackout. On tape we hear the radio—*BICKWOOD *and* LEWIS.)

BICKWOOD: Wasn't that the dandiest little love song you ever heard?

LEWIS: It was.

BICKWOOD: It sure was.

LEWIS: Pass that record over here. I want to take it home to my wife.

(We hear the sound of a needle scraping across a record.)

BICKWOOD: Sorry about that.

LEWIS: Never mind. I'll buy the tape.

BICKWOOD: Well, I guess that's it for today. Who's comin' up now?

LEWIS: Lemmee see . . . Wilbur Rensnitch will be reading his essay that won all the prizes in the Bedford Creek High School contest. It's called "Toxic Waste: Looking on the Bright Side." What a timely topic it is.

BICKWOOD: It is. And then what?

LEWIS: Then we'll play the national anthem and go home.

BICKWOOD: It sounds good. Let's do it and get out of here.

LEWIS: Gone, gone, gone. So, somebody go get Wilbur. I'm gettin' antsy.

BICKWOOD *(shouting away from the microphone)*: Wilbur—get your essay in here!

LEWIS: I'm Lewis.

BICKWOOD: And I'm Bickwood, and this has been Lewis and Bickwood on WCOW—in the heart of Bedford Creek . . .

Epilogue

(Lights up on the cabin. It is virtually empty—except for a few pieces of furniture it started out with. It is a week later. BETH, *followed by* DAVID, *enters with their luggage.* DAVID *takes hers out of her hands.)*

DAVID: I'll take that. The doctor said you shouldn't carry anything.

BETH: Thank you, kind sir.

DAVID: You're welcome, my lady. *(Puts luggage down, looks around)* Take a good look. This'll probably be the last time you see this place.

BETH *(shaking her head with disbelief)*: I can't believe your dad's selling it—after all that work.

DAVID: He said it outlived its usefulness. Escape is nice only if you're escaping from the right things.

BETH: Did he say that?

DAVID: I paraphrased.

BETH: Your father can be wise sometimes.

DAVID: It was *my* paraphrase.

BETH: You can be wise sometimes, too, dear. *(She kisses him lightly)* David . . . will you forgive me?

DAVID: What? Are you crazy? I'm the one who's been the jerk. Why should I need to forgive you?

BETH: For locking you in a suit of white armor. For trying to live a fairy tale.

DAVID: Beth . . .

(She kisses him. He pulls her closer for a heartfelt embrace. MARK *enters.)*

MARK: Oh, brother. Are you two at it again?

DAVID: Take notes, little man.

(He kisses BETH *again.)*

MARK: Stop it. You're contributing to the delinquency of a minor. Dad said to hurry up. He wants to avoid the traffic going home.

(JIM *enters hurriedly,* CHARLIE *follows, looking over a document of some sort.*)

CHARLIE: Jim, are you *sure* about this?

JIM: How sure do I have to be? Come on, let's get this luggage loaded.

CHARLIE: But—

JIM (*turns to her*): Yes, Charlie. It's what I want to do. You were right in the beginning.

(MATTY *and* SAMSON *enter. This time* MATTY *is wearing an old-fashioned lifeguard outfit and* SAMSON *is dressed, well, like* SAMSON.)

MATTY: Hi, gang. Look, I don't have a lot of time. The kids can't go in the pool till I get there. What do I have to sign?

(CHARLIE *gives her the papers.*)

MARK: What are those—your walking papers?

MATTY (*signing the papers*): It's a contract.

MARK: On whose life?

MATTY: On the cabin, smart boy.

MARK: You're joking.

JIM (*shrugs*): She wants to buy it as an investment.

DAVID: *This?* An investment?

MARK: I'll bet she has stock in Edsels, too.

JIM: Matty, if you don't want to do it—

MATTY: Don't be foolish. Take the money and run. This is a nice cabin. You folks put a lot of life into it.

CHARLIE: Not to mention two marriages. (MATTY *hands the papers back to* CHARLIE.)

MATTY: Thank you. And God bless.

JIM (*claps hands*): OK! That's it! Let's rock and roll out of here!

(*They grab the remaining luggage, saying good-byes and fond hugs farewell and exit —except for* MATTY, *who drifts downstage to address the audience.*)

MATTY: See? Things just don't happen the way you think they will. But don't go getting the wrong idea. Happy endings don't come this easy. No sirree . . . a year has gone by and Jim and Charlie—and even David and Beth—are still working everything out . . . much to their surprise. Maybe they thought God would fix everything overnight. Maybe you think so, too. He doesn't always do it that way. And Mark? He got accepted to the university but wound up going to junior college because it was the only thing he could afford. He's become a pretty resourceful businessman. He was trying to raise money by sponsoring mud wrestling fights in the moat in their backyard . . . but Charlie put a stop to it. So you see, things just don't always work out the way we think they will. I bought the cabin from the Baileys and when we had our first big rain, the roof fell in. That's OK. Samson fixed it in no time for the summer tourists and Dale Johnson got it rented right away . . . to the Baileys. No . . . happy endings don't come real easy and not always as quick as we'd like. But they do come if we take what the good Lord tells us to do and work at it. See you soon.

(MATTY *exits as the lights fade to blackout.*)